Out of the Dark

Coping with Emotional Challenges

ABDO
Publishing Company

Strong, Beautiful Girls

Out of the Dark

Coping with Emotional Challenges

by Amanda Doering Tourville

Content Consultant
Dr. Robyn J. A. Silverman
Child/Teen Development Expert and Success Coach
Powerful Words Character Development

Credits

Published by ABDO Publishing Company, 8000 West 78th Street, Edina, Minnesota 55439. Copyright © 2010 by Abdo Consulting Group, Inc. International copyrights reserved in all countries. No part of this book may be reproduced in any form without written permission from the publisher. The Essential Library™ is a trademark and logo of ABDO Publishing Company.

Printed in the United States.

Editor: Melissa Johnson
Copy Editor: Amy Van Zee
Interior Design and Production: Becky Daum
Cover Design: Becky Daum

Library of Congress Cataloging-in-Publication Data
Tourville, Amanda Doering, 1980-
  Out of the dark : coping with emotional challenges / by Amanda Doering Tourville ; content Consultant, Robyn J. A. Silverman.
    p. cm. — (Essential health : strong, beautiful girls)
  Includes index.
  ISBN 978-1-60453-752-9
  1. Emotional problems of teenagers. 2. Emotional problems of children. 3. Teenage girls—Psychology. 4. Girls—Psychology. I. Title.

BF723.E598T68 2010
155.5'33—dc22
                              2009002135

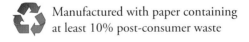 Manufactured with paper containing at least 10% post-consumer waste

Contents

Meet Dr. Robyn 6

Take It from Me 8

Chapter 1. On the Move. 10

Chapter 2. Out of Focus 18

Chapter 3. No Magic Pill 28

Chapter 4. The Blues. 38

Chapter 5. The Worry Girl 48

Chapter 6. Not Enough Love 56

Chapter 7. The Breakup 66

Chapter 8. Girl's Best Friend. 74

Chapter 9. A Tragic End 82

Chapter 10. Losing Dad. 92

A Second Look 102

Pay It Forward 104

Additional Resources. 106

Glossary. 108

Index 110

About the Author 112

Meet Dr. Robyn

Dr. Robyn Silverman loves to spend time with young people. It's what she does best! As a child and adolescent development specialist, Dr. Robyn has devoted her time to helping girls just like you become all they can be. Throughout the Strong, Beautiful Girls series, you'll hear her expert advice as she offers wisdom on boyfriends, school, and everything in between.

An award-winning body image expert and the creator of the Powerful Words Character System, Dr. Robyn likes to look on the bright side of life. She knows how tough it is to be a young woman in today's world, and she's prepared with encouragement to help you embrace your beauty even when your "frenemies" tell you otherwise. Dr. Robyn struggled with her own body image while growing up, so she knows what you're going through.

Dr. Robyn has been told she has a rare talent—to help girls share their wildest dreams and biggest problems. Her compassion makes her a trusted friend to many girls, and she considers it a gift to be able to interact with the young people who she sees as the leaders of tomorrow. She even started a girls' group, the Sassy Sisterhood Girls Circle, to help young women pinpoint how media messages impact their lives and body confidence so they can get

As a speaker and a success coach, her powerful messages have reached thousands of people. Her expert advice has been featured in *Prevention* magazine, *Parents* magazine, and the *Washington Post*. She was even a guest editor for the Dove Self-Esteem Fund: Campaign for Real Beauty. But she has an online presence too, and her writing can be found through her blogs, www.DrRobynsBlog.com and www.BodyImageBlog.com, or through her Web site, www.DrRobynSilverman.com. Dr. Robyn also enjoys spending time with her family in Massachusetts.

Dr. Robyn believes that young people are assets to be developed, not problems to be fixed. She's out to help you become the best you can be. As she puts it, "I'm stepping up to the plate to highlight news stories gone wrong, girls gone right, and programs that help to support strengths instead of weaknesses. I'd be grateful if you'd join me."

Take It from Me

The topics in this book are heavy, difficult issues to address. The middle-school years are emotional anyway with the changes taking place in your body and in your mind. If that isn't enough, some girls have to deal with traumatic problems including depression, substance abuse, or the death of a loved one. These are difficult for people of any age to cope with.

In many ways, I was the typical middle-school girl. I worried about wearing the right clothes, spent as much time as I could with friends, and had my first serious crushes. I had the same hopes and fears as most girls my age. What most girls my age weren't dealing with, though, were depression and anxiety. I remember my first panic attack vividly. I was 11 years old, and it was the middle of the night. My breathing became labored, my body shook uncontrollably, and my mind raced with horrifying thoughts. It was the most terrifying thing I had ever experienced.

My depression and anxiety grew worse as I got older. My anxiety caused me to be afraid to go on medication. Instead, I tried herbal supplements, diet and exercise, and therapy. While these all helped, they weren't enough for me. Finally, I realized that I shouldn't be ashamed to go on medication. I hadn't done anything wrong to "deserve" depression and anxiety. In fact, I deserved to get the help I needed. My doctor diagnosed me with clinical depression and gave me antidepressants. I'd like to say that medication completely cured me, but I'd be lying. What I can tell you is that when I went on medication, my life definitely changed for the better.

I carried shame at being depressed and anxious because I thought it somehow made me weak, or a less capable human being. This couldn't be further from the truth. As I've grown older, I've been shocked to learn that some of the smartest, most creative, competent people I have ever met struggle with depression and anxiety. I've learned that it's often the struggles that we survive that make us who we are. The hope is that these emotionally trying experiences make us stronger, smarter, more compassionate people.

I sincerely hope that this book will give you the knowledge and courage to take on your emotional issues. Please remember, though, that many emotional issues should be discussed with an adult who can help you work through your feelings, and if needed, get you additional help. You shouldn't take on these burdens by yourself, and you don't have to.

XOXO,
Amanda

1

On the Move

The words "we're moving" can be the most dreaded thing a girl can hear. Being a preteen or teenage girl is difficult enough without adding the adjustments of a new home, new friends, a new school, or a new town. A move can change nearly everything.

Moving can be a good thing, though. Sometimes there are bad memories in a home or town, especially in cases of divorce or other traumatic experiences. Moving can mean a fresh start and new opportunities for the entire family.

A move will definitely cause mixed feelings. While a move may be a new beginning, it can be very sad to leave family, friends, and schools. A new environment can be exciting and scary at the same time. This mixture of feelings is normal. The adjustment may be tough, but there will be positive aspects to the changes as well. Padma wasn't looking forward to her family's move.

Padma's Story

Padma lived in a small town in Illinois and knew almost everyone in it. She had grown up with most of the kids in her class and had been friends with many of them since before she could remember. She took riding lessons at a stable outside of town. Padma felt safe in her neighborhood, and all the buildings and roads of her town were familiar to her. She thought she would live there forever.

One day, Padma's parents told her they would be moving. Padma's mother had gotten a promotion at work, and she would have to move to California. California was a long way away from Padma's small town, and she had never been there before.

"California!" Padma exclaimed. She was shocked by the news. "Why do we have to go?"

"This is a wonderful opportunity for your mother," said Padma's dad. "This is the job she's worked so hard for. I know moving will be tough, but it's what's best for our family."

"But what about me? What about my friends? What about my riding? I bet there are no horses in California!" said Padma.

A new environment can be exciting and scary at the same time.

Her mother smiled and put an arm around Padma. "Of course there are horses in California. We'll find a riding stable as soon as we get there. As for your friends, it will be tough to leave them, but you can always e-mail and talk on the phone. And you'll make lots of new friends, too."

Talk About It

- Have you ever moved? What was it like? How did you feel?

- What are some of the reasons families move?

Padma's parents told her they would be living outside a large city. That scared Padma. She wasn't used to big cities and skyscrapers. Her parents took her to Chicago once, and the noise and tall buildings made her head spin. She liked her peaceful small town. Padma worried that she wouldn't be able to make new friends, and she worried about fitting in. At the same time, she also wondered what her new life would be like.

Padma felt sad, excited, angry, and scared about moving—sometimes all in one day! She was sad to leave her house, her friends, and her town. She was excited to see California and to live in a warm place. She was angry that her parents were making her move. She was scared that she wouldn't like her new neighborhood or make new friends.

Padma's last day at school was the hardest of all.

Moving was stressful. Every item Padma packed made the move a little more real for her. She cried as she packed up her room. She couldn't believe that the next time she saw her things, they would be in California.

Padma's last day at school was the hardest of all. She hated leaving her friends and her teachers. She couldn't believe that she may never see some of them again. The thought made her feel lonely and sad. Her friends promised to e-mail and call, but everyone knew it wouldn't be the same.

Talk About It

- **Why is Padma concerned about making new friends?**

- **If you were moving, what would be your biggest fears?**

- **Why do Padma and her friends know that calling and e-mailing won't be the same as being together?**

That evening, Padma broke down. "Why are you making us leave?" she screamed at her mom. She was so happy where she was. Why did her mom have to uproot them now?

Padma's mom held her close. Padma sobbed on her shoulder. "I know this is tough, Padma. It's tough for your father and me, too. We'll get through this as a family, though. I know it seems like everything is changing, but the most important thing, our family, is staying the same."

Padma knew that what her mom was saying was true. The next few months would be hard on all of them, but they would face the move together. They could rely on each other for comfort and strength.

Talk About It

- Why was Padma angry with her mother?

- What will change about Padma's life when she moves? What will stay the same?

- What advice would you give to Padma about moving?

Moving can be a very emotional and stressful time for a family. Change is always a little fright- ening, and moving means a lot of changes.

Many girls faced with moving worry about losing their friends. Phone calls, e-mails, tex- ting, picture messaging, and social networking Web sites are ways to stay involved in your friends' lives. Some of your friendships may change or gradually fade. This is natural, and it doesn't mean you did anything wrong. Friends grow and change, and sometimes they move on—even when nobody moves out of town.

Girls who change schools or move to a new town also worry about making new friends. It may be tough at first, but by getting involved in school, community, or religious activities, you will meet new people with the same interests and values that you have. Just be yourself and you will make friends just as you've made friends before.

If your family is moving, you may be feeling a lot of emotions. You're probably sad, a little angry, a little excited, and kind of scared about the future. These are all normal feelings. Your parents may be very busy during the move, but it is important that you talk to them about how you feel. Chances are, they are feeling the same emotions you are!

Get Healthy

1. Take photographs of your house and your neighborhood. Write memories in your journal to remember after the move.

2. Talk to your friends about what will happen if one of you moves. Have a plan for how you will stay in touch.

3. Focus on the positive. Research some things about your new hometown—museums, shopping malls, restaurants, or other nearby attractions. When you arrive, get a parent or a sibling to explore with you.

The Last Word from Amanda

Moving during this time in your life can be very difficult and stressful. It's hard to leave your friends, your home, and your familiar routines. It will take time, but you will adjust to your new surroundings. Life may even be better in your new environment.

Moving is tough, but it isn't all bad. Think about the good things about your move. How will you decorate your new room? Maybe you'll have a bigger backyard, or have more nature around you. Try to think of your move as a fresh start. This is your opportunity to meet new people, learn about new places, and have new adventures.

2

Out of Focus

We've all spaced out in a boring class or had a hard time paying attention when we have something on our minds. We may feel impatient or antsy sometimes. We've all said or done inappropriate things at the wrong time every once in a while. For people with Attention Deficit Hyperactivity Disorder (ADHD), difficulty paying attention, restlessness, and acting without thinking are a part of life.

ADHD affects every aspect of life. Kids with ADHD often have a difficult time in school because they are easily distracted and have trouble focusing. ADHD can make friendships and family life more challenging. Although ADHD is considered a behavior disorder, it can have emotional effects. Read Kyla's story to see how she deals with having ADHD.

Kyla's Story

Kyla often wondered why life seemed so hard for her. She had a tough time in school, and she always seemed to be getting into trouble. Home wasn't so great either. She was always forgetting to do her chores or doing a sloppy job when she did do them. She didn't mean to be a problem, but she had difficulty concentrating and focusing on tasks.

She didn't mean to be a problem, but she had difficulty concentrating and focusing on tasks.

Kyla was always fidgeting. She didn't like to sit still, which was another reason she got into trouble at school. She would look for any excuse to get up from her seat.

"Kyla, please sit down," said Mrs. Alder, her English teacher. "You're supposed to be reading."

Kyla didn't like reading. It was boring. She went back to her seat, but scribbled a note to her friend, Holly. She passed the note to Anna, who sat next to Holly. Anna gave Kyla a dirty look, but tried passing the note along to Holly.

"Anna, Holly, what are you two doing?" said Mrs. Alder. "You need to be reading, not passing notes." Mrs. Alder took the note from Anna and crumpled it

in her hand. Now, both Anna and Holly were glaring at Kyla.

"Sorry!" whispered Kyla. The two girls turned back to their reading. Kyla leaned back in her seat and blew her bangs out of her eyes. Would this class ever be over?

After class, Kyla overheard Holly and Anna talking.

"I mean, Kyla's my friend, but sometimes she doesn't know when to stop! It's not fair that I get into trouble because she's doing stupid things," said Holly.

"Yeah, I know," said Anna. "She doesn't seem to think before she does stuff."

Kyla pushed past the two girls. "Geez, I said I was sorry," Kyla said, walking away.

Talk About It

- Do you know anyone with ADHD? If so, do they act differently from other people their age?

- Why were Anna and Holly upset with Kyla? Do you agree with them?

- How do you think Kyla felt when she overheard her friends talking about her? Have you ever overheard a friend talking about you?

That evening, Kyla's parents asked to talk to her. They had received a call from Kyla's math teacher, Mr. Dorset. Kyla hadn't turned in the last four homework assignments.

"Kyla, this is the second call we've received from Mr. Dorset this quarter!" said Kyla's mom. "Why aren't you keeping up in his class? He says you don't pay attention and you fidget all the time."

Kyla squirmed in her seat. "I'm sorry, Mom! I hate math," she said.

Kyla's mom sighed. "You hate school altogether, Kyla. Why? I know you're a smart girl. You're just not applying yourself."

"Kyla," her dad said, "there will be no video games, cell phone, or friends until these assignments are turned in. Do you understand?" Kyla nodded.

She didn't know how she'd get through those assignments. Kyla hadn't done them because she didn't

understand how to do the problems. She didn't understand how to do the problems because she hadn't been
paying attention in class.

"And you forgot to feed Chipper last night. He
was starving this morning when I came downstairs,"
said Kyla's mom. Chipper was the family's golden
retriever.

"Oops," said Kyla. "Sorry, Chipper." Kyla felt bad
about not feeding the dog. She had forgotten to feed
him before, but she usually caught it before anyone
else did.

Kyla felt sad that night. It seemed like she was
always apologizing for things she didn't mean to do.
School was a disaster, Holly was mad at her for getting

her in trouble, and she couldn't even remember to feed the dog. What was wrong with her?

Talk About It

- **Have you ever fallen behind in school because you didn't pay attention in class? If so, what did you do about it?**

- **What kind of emotions do you think Kyla is feeling?**

After school the next day, Kyla's mom appeared in the hallway. "Kyla, I was called to meet with your teacher, Mrs. Alder, and the school counselor. Do you know what this is about?"

Kyla shrugged. With the way things were going, it could be anything.

Kyla and her mom went to the conference room and sat down with Mrs. Alder and Mr. Holmes, the guidance counselor.

"Kyla, Mrs. Curtis, thank you for coming in today," said Mr. Holmes. "I'll get right to the point. Kyla has

"Kyla, I was called to meet with your teacher, Mrs. Alder, and the school counselor. Do you know what this is about?"

been having some issues in school lately. Her teachers are concerned about her lack of focus in class. We'd like to have her evaluated."

Kyla went to see a specialist. After several sessions, it was clear: Kyla had ADHD. The specialist prescribed medication and therapy sessions to help her change her behavior. At first, Kyla was really worried about the medicine. She was afraid the medicine might change her personality or that she'd stop acting like herself.

After a few months on medication, Kyla was doing better in school and at home. She was getting back on track in class, and she wasn't getting herself or her friends into trouble as often as before. And, she even remembered to take care of Chipper! She was still completely herself—she had just found her focus.

Talk About It

- Have you ever had to meet with your parents and the guidance counselor? If so, about what?

- Do you take any medication? How do you feel about taking it?

ADHD affects 8 to 10 percent of all children and teens, making it the most diagnosed behavior disorder in kids. Three basic characteristics make up ADHD: inattention, hyperactivity, and impulsivity. ADHD is also closely connected with depression and anxiety, although it can exist without these disorders.

Kids with ADHD find it difficult to concentrate and are easily distracted. They daydream or zone out when they should be listening. They may forget to do homework or chores and tend to be disorganized.

When a person is hyperactive, it means he or she is overactive and always moving. Hyperactive people have a hard time sitting still. They feel restless and may feel the need to be physically busy at all times.

Impulsivity is doing or saying something without thinking of the consequences. People with ADHD have trouble controlling their urges. They often blurt out inappropriate comments or interrupt people while they are talking. They may talk all the time, even when they know they shouldn't. Their impulsive actions tend to get them into trouble.

If these descriptions sound like things that you deal with, you may have ADHD. Talk to a parent or another trusted adult. A doctor can diagnose ADHD and set up a treatment plan that may include medication and/or behavioral therapy.

Get Healthy

1. If you have trouble concentrating on homework, turn off e-mail, instant messaging, and your cell phone, if you have one.

2. Get organized! If you have trouble remembering to do certain things, use a daily planner or a notebook to write down all the things you need to do. Ask for help getting organized if you need it.

3. If you think you might have ADHD, make sure to exercise. Exercise can help calm you and focus your mind. If you have trouble sitting still, take short breaks when working on large tasks.

The Last Word from Amanda

Life with ADHD can be tough, but there is help. Talk to your parents or your doctor if you are concerned about having ADHD. Medication can help you feel calmer, and therapy can teach you how to cope with the disorder. Many of the skills that are taught in therapy are things everyone needs to know eventually. With treatment, you can live a normal life. Who knows—you may just end up ahead of the game!

3

No Magic Pill

Have you ever wished there were a magic pill that would solve all your problems? Society has led us to believe that various substances can make us thinner, smarter, happier, and more popular. Every day we are bombarded by advertisements and television shows with beautiful people sipping colorful drinks at cool parties. Every weight-loss advertisement promises to make us look like swimsuit models if we take that product. Even prescription drug advertisements show people made better by simply popping a pill. The real truth is that there is no pill, powder, or drink that can make us look perfect or feel good all the time.

Kids experiment and abuse substances for many reasons. Some kids are curious about how they will feel on certain substances. Some kids smoke, drink alcohol, take drugs, or abuse prescription medication because they think using these things makes them cool. Some think they can escape their problems through substances. Others think abusing pills, powders, or drinks will help them get ahead in school or sports. Some kids try to cope with depression, anxiety, or other disorders by abusing substances. In fact, people who suffer from depression are more likely to abuse substances such as alcohol, drugs, and prescription medications.

Some kids try to cope with depression, anxiety, or other disorders by abusing substances.

Not everyone who experiments with alcohol or drugs will end up abusing these substances, but why take the risk? Valerie thought that taking a prescription medication would be a one-time thing, but she couldn't stop after just one use.

Valerie's Story

Valerie was failing math. No matter how hard she tried to study, she couldn't focus for more than a few minutes. With swimming practice and meets after school and drama club on the weekends, she barely had enough time to do her homework. Math was always left until last, when she was so tired she could barely keep her eyes open.

Valerie had to find some way to pass the last test of the semester. If she failed, she would be kicked off the swim team.

After swim practice, Valerie approached Mei, an older girl on the team. "Hey, Mei, that was a great practice. Your form looked really good."

Mei toweled off her hair. "Thanks, Valerie. Yours looked good, too."

"Not really," said Valerie. "I'm having trouble with my turns. I want to practice more, but I have so much homework!"

"Just wait until eighth grade," laughed Mei.

"I can barely keep up now. I'm failing math," Valerie admitted.

"Yeah, Mr. Pearson is tough. I almost failed his class, too," said Mei.

"How did you pass?" asked Valerie.

Mei smiled. "Let's just say I had a little help." She pulled out a little orange bottle of pills from her backpack. "One of these should help you study." She handed the bottle to Valerie.

"What is it?" asked Valerie.

"Some medication my little brother takes," replied Mei.

Valerie had heard of kids who took prescription drugs that weren't theirs. The pills helped them study, gave them more energy, or just made them feel good. Valerie thought that taking someone else's pills was silly, maybe even dangerous. But if it could help her pass this test, she thought it might be worth a try.

Valerie thought that taking someone else's pills was silly, maybe even dangerous.

"Is it safe?" Valerie asked Mei.

Mei shrugged. "It's a prescribed medication. It's not like I'm taking heroin."

Valerie giggled nervously. "Yeah, I guess so."

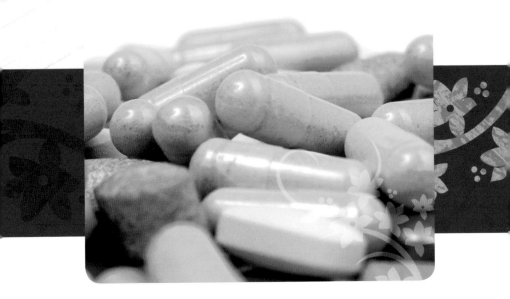

Talk About It

- Do you know anyone who abuses alcohol or drugs? Why do you think they abuse substances?

- What are the risks of taking medication that isn't prescribed for you?

That night, Valerie took the pill Mei had given her. After an hour, she felt a slight buzz in her head. At 10:30 p.m., she started her math homework. She was able to get through all of the problems and even got the right answers on some of them. It was amazing! It was nearly 3:00 a.m. before she went to sleep.

The next day, Valerie found Mei after practice. "I need some more pills," Valerie told her. "The test is next Thursday, and I'll need to study from now until then if I plan on passing."

"Whoa, slow down," said Mei. "You're not supposed to take it every day. Only when you need it."

"I definitely need it," said Valerie. Mei handed her the pills.

Talk About It

- **Why do you think Valerie felt she needed the pills?**

- **Have you ever felt like you needed to take something to study or stay up late? What did you do in that situation?**

Valerie took the pills every night and stayed up late studying. She felt great while the pills were working, but she was tired and run down later when they wore off.

On Saturday, Valerie slept late. Her mom jostled her awake at 11:30 a.m. "Valerie, you'll be late to drama club if you don't hurry," said her mom. Valerie was so tired she could barely open her eyes.

"I'm not going, Mom," she muttered. "I'm too tired to move."

"You don't look so good, either," said Valerie's mom. "You're so pale, and there are dark circles under your eyes." Valerie rolled over and put the pillow over her head.

Valerie's swim coach, Ms. Carver, noticed the change in Valerie, too. She wasn't swimming as well as she usually did, and Ms. Carver told her so.

"I'm just tired from studying," Valerie said. "I promise I'll be better next week."

The day before her big test, Valerie fell asleep in math class. Mr. Pearson asked her to stay after class.

"Valerie, you don't seem to be your usual self," said Mr. Pearson.

"I'm fine," Valerie replied. "Just a little tired."

"Well, I hope you'll be rested for tomorrow's test. You know that this test will determine whether you pass the class," said Mr. Pearson.

Valerie sighed. "I know," she said quietly.

Talk About It

- Why was Valerie so tired?
- Should Valerie's mother and teachers have done something to help her? If so, what?

That night, Valerie took a pill and began studying. Her head buzzed with energy. Around 4:00 a.m., she finally fell asleep. The next morning, Valerie was exhausted. Her head hurt, and she felt queasy. She couldn't be sick today. She had to pass that test! Shortly before math class, Valerie popped two of the pills into her mouth, thinking that if one pill was good, two would definitely be better.

The first few problems of the test went well, but then Valerie's heart started racing. She felt light-headed and sick to her stomach.

The next thing she knew, Valerie woke up in a strange bed. There were machines hooked up to her arm. Her mother was crying quietly in the corner, holding the bottle of pills from Valerie's bag. Valerie knew instantly that her swim season was over.

Talk About It

- What did Valerie gain by using unprescribed medication? What did she lose?

- How else could Valerie have passed the test without using drugs?

- How do you think Valerie felt when she woke up in the hospital? What do you think will happen to her?

Because alcohol and street drugs can be expensive and difficult to get, some kids abuse prescription medications, which can often be found in their homes' medicine cabinets. Some kids may think that because these medicines are prescribed, they are safer to take. This is not true. Medication is very specific to the person it is prescribed for. Taking medication that is not yours puts you at risk for emotional problems, physical sickness, addiction, and even death. Taking a medication that has not been prescribed for you is not only dangerous—it's also illegal. You can be held legally responsible for taking another person's medication.

Experimentation with drugs or alcohol can lead to substance abuse. Substance abuse can lead to dependence or addiction. The user then needs the substance to function or needs to use more of the substance to get the same effects as when she first started using the drugs. Stay healthy and stay away from drugs and medications that aren't yours.

Get Healthy

1. If you or a friend has a problem with substance abuse, get help! Talk to a parent, school counselor, coach, or other trusted adult. The sooner you get help, the sooner you can get clean and stay clean.

2. Make a list of all the fun things you can do without abusing substances. If and when you are tempted to use drugs or alcohol, do one of these things instead.

3. If you are on a prescription medication, follow the directions exactly. Never give your medication to anyone else for any reason.

4. If you're feeling overwhelmed by school or by other commitments, talk to a trusted adult about finding a better balance. Turning to illegal substances is never the answer.

The Last Word from Amanda

Your life is filled with pressure and stress from friends, school, extracurricular activities, and family. It can be tempting to try to escape these pressures by getting drunk, popping a pill, or smoking a joint. What often happens, though, is that substances interfere with our ability to make good decisions.

Maybe you haven't been tempted to use substances or been faced with the choice of using them. That's good. Decide right now to say no if you run into a situation where substances are present. If you have experimented with substances, make the decision to stop right now and encourage your friends to do the same.

4

The Blues

*W*e've all felt sad or blue at times. We've had a fight with a friend, bombed an important test, or had to make a difficult change. I remember crying myself to sleep every night during the first week of sixth grade. I was in a much bigger school and didn't have any of my old friends in my classes. I didn't think I would ever make new friends. After a few weeks, I made new friends, kept my old friends, and slept peacefully the rest of the year. These situational kinds of depression are normal and generally pass before too long. But how do we know if what we're feeling is something more, something bigger and scarier than we can handle?

What if everything seems like it should be great—you have plenty of friends and you're doing well in school—but you just aren't happy? Some girls go through periods of sadness, where everything seems bleak and hopeless. Sometimes girls cry for no reason or feel like life just isn't worth living. Abby felt worthless, sad, and tired all the time. Read on to see how Abby's parents intervened in her depression.

Abby's Story

Abby was bummed. Things were going okay, she guessed, but something wasn't quite right, something she couldn't quite put her finger on. For the most part, life was good, but Abby was still sad.

Abby had been sad before, of course. She cried when her pet guinea pig died, and she was upset when she got into a big **Abby felt worthless, sad, and tired all the time.** fight with her best friend, Madison, last year. But this was different. She didn't know why she was sad. She just was.

Abby used to love playing soccer. She was in the school choir and had always enjoyed shopping and sleepovers with her friends. But now, she didn't feel like doing anything. Just getting up, showering, and going to school were hard enough. She felt tired all the time, but she couldn't sleep at night.

The only thing that Abby wanted to do was eat. It seemed to make her feel better . . . for a while, at least.

She had gained 15 pounds in the past few months. With the added weight and constant tiredness, Abby could barely make it through soccer practice anymore.

Talk About It

- **How is Abby's sadness now different from when she was sad about losing her guinea pig and fighting with her friend?**

- **Have you ever been sad for no reason? If so, did you think it was depression?**

- **Why do you think Abby eats all the time? Have you ever eaten because you were sad?**

"What's up with you lately?" Madison asked Abby one day after soccer practice. "You seem out of it."

Abby sighed. She was sick of her parents, friends, and teachers asking what was wrong. "Nothing's up. I'm just tired, that's all," she said.

"Do you want to come over for dinner? We could practice our penalty kicks after we eat," said Madison.

Abby paused. She was sick of playing soccer. "Nah, I've got too much homework," she lied.

"Okay. Sondra's birthday party is on Saturday. Maybe you can spend the night," suggested Madison.

"Yeah, we'll see," said Abby.

Talk About It

- Why do you think Abby lied to Madison about having too much homework?

- If you were Madison, what would you say to Abby?

Abby watched television all day Saturday. She didn't really want to go to the party. She didn't want to do anything.

"Honey, you'd better get showered and dressed. The party starts in an hour," said Abby's mom. Abby dragged herself off the couch and got into the shower. What was wrong with her lately? She used to love parties. Now, she dreaded them. The parties hadn't changed. Something had changed in her. This is so stupid, Abby thought. Why can't I just be happy like I used to be?

Abby got out of the shower and began dressing. She grabbed a pair of new jeans, but they were too tight around the waist. The next pair she found didn't fit either. Frustrated, Abby threw the clothes on the floor and climbed into bed. The tears began to well up, and before she knew it, Abby was sobbing loudly.

Abby's mom rushed into the room. "Abby, what's wrong?" Abby couldn't talk through her tears. Abby's mom held her. After a few minutes, Abby's mom said, "Abby, you'll be late for the party."

"I'm not going," Abby mumbled.

"Why not?" asked Abby's mom. "Sondra will be so disappointed if you're not there. What's really wrong, Abby?"

Abby thought for a minute. "I don't know, Mom," she sniffed. "I really don't know."

Talk About It

- **Why do you think Abby doesn't want to go to Sondra's party?**
- **Why doesn't Abby know what's wrong with her?**

Abby's mom helped her find an outfit and curled her hair. Abby was only a few minutes late to the party. She even had a good time, although she worried that she didn't seem happy enough.

The next day, Abby's parents had a talk with her. They had noticed that she wasn't the same happy, active girl she had been. They wanted to know if anything was wrong. Abby sat in silence for a few moments. "I don't know what's wrong. I'm just not happy anymore," she told her parents, tears running down her cheeks.

"Honey, we think you may be depressed," Abby's dad said.

"But there's no reason for me to be depressed," countered Abby.

"Sometimes there's no reason to be sad, but you still are," explained Abby's mom. "It's not your fault, Abby. You didn't do anything wrong to cause it."

"How can I make it go away?" asked Abby. She felt like she was going to start crying again.

"Sometimes there's no reason to be sad, but you still are," explained Abby's mom.

"We'd like to take you to the doctor. She can see what we can do to help you feel better. Does that sound like a good plan?" her dad asked.

Abby nodded. Her parents hugged her. Abby felt a little better already.

Talk About It

- Why do you think Abby had a good time at the party even though she didn't want to go?

- Do you think Abby's parents were right to approach her about depression?

- Why do you think talking to her parents made Abby feel better?

There are two kinds of depression. Situationa
depression is when you have feelings of sadness for a reason. A fight with your parents, a
bad grade at school, or problems with friends
can cause you to feel sad or hurt. These feelings
usually go away in minutes, hours, or days.

Clinical depression, on the other hand, is
when a traumatic event or the chemical makeup of the brain causes prolonged feelings of
sadness, worthlessness, irritability, changes
in sleep patterns or appetite, or even thoughts
of suicide or self-harm. Events that can cause
prolonged depression include witnessing or
being the victim of a violent crime, your parents
divorcing, or the death of a family member. In
other cases, the imbalance of the chemicals
that run through a person's brain causes them
to be depressed. This type of depression is
often passed down genetically through
families.

If you think you may be suffering from
clinical depression, the important thing to
remember is that there is help. Tell your parents or another trusted adult how you feel. Be
honest with them and don't try to hide your
feelings, even if those feelings are scary. Your
parents should take you to see a doctor who
can evaluate, diagnose, and treat you

Get Healthy

1. If you think you might be clinically depressed, get help! Talk about your feelings with someone you trust. Just talking about it may help you feel better. If it's not enough, see your doctor. He or she may prescribe counseling, therapy, and/or medication.

2. Many people with depression don't feel like doing anything, but being a couch potato is the worst thing you can do. Hang out with friends, play a game with your family, or ride your bike outside. Doing activities that you enjoy will improve your mood.

3. Exercise and diet can help you cope with depression. Make sure to get 30 to 60 minutes of exercise a day and maintain a nutritious diet.

The Last Word from Amanda

The preteen and teenage years are hard enough on girls. Depression only adds to the difficult job of growing up. There is no shame in seeking help for clinical depression. Medication and therapy to change the way you react to negative thoughts can improve depression symptoms or relieve these symptoms entirely. You owe it to yourself to get the help you need. Life is an amazing adventure. Don't let depression get in the way of living it to the fullest.

5

The Worry Girl

ave you ever had butterflies in your stomach before going onstage or felt anxious before a big test? A little nervousness is perfectly normal and healthy. But what if you felt anxious all the time? What if that anxiety kept you from seeing your friends? What if you always felt nervous about the future? Anxiety disorders can cause people of all ages to fear and dread normal, everyday experiences.

While the two disorders can be experienced separately, depression and anxiety are very closely linked. Many people with anxiety are also depressed. Many people who are depressed are also anxious. It makes sense, because these two emotional issues create a vicious circle of worry and sadness. Maria found herself worrying about everything, and it was really starting to cause problems.

Maria's Story

Maria was a worrier. Her parents laughed because at a young age, she worried about things that no little girl should worry about. When Maria was four, she worried about the squirrels during the winter months. She was sure that when she was cold, they were, too. When she was six and her older brother failed a math test, she was certain that she would do poorly at math, too.

School was very difficult for Maria. She became very nervous before tests, no matter how much she had studied. Her palms would sweat, and her heart would race. She couldn't concentrate on the questions.

As she got older, Maria's worry turned into fear. She began to fear that bad things would happen to her, to her family, or to her friends. After her mom got into a car accident, Maria cried for months when her mom would leave to go to work. Many days, Maria did not want to leave the house.

Her palms would sweat, and her heart would race. She couldn't concentrate on the questions.

Talk About It

- Why do you think Maria's parents laughed about her worries when she was a child?

- Have you ever been so nervous about a test that it was difficult for you to concentrate? What happened?

Because she was always afraid, Maria avoided new experiences. When her sixth grade class went skiing, Maria sat in the chalet. Her friends begged her to try the bunny hill, but Maria wouldn't budge. She pictured herself with broken arms and legs and began to tremble.

Maria sat alone in the chalet, watching her friends through the window. They zoomed down the bunny hill, laughing and spraying each other with snow as they stopped. They were having so much fun. A tear trickled down Maria's cheek. It wasn't fair! Why were they able to race down the hill without a care, when the thought of riding the chair lift was enough to make Maria's stomach turn? In fact, the more she thought of the chair lift, the more she felt like throwing up. She wanted to be out there skiing with them, but the overwhelming fear and worry kept her firmly planted in her seat.

Maria sat alone in the chalet, watching her friends through the window.

On the bus ride home, her classmates chattered about their skiing experiences. Maria was quiet. Stephen, one of the class bullies, suddenly singled her out. "Hey, Maria, what hills did you go down? Oh, yeah, I forgot. You were watching the chalet, making sure it didn't walk away."

Some of Maria's classmates giggled, and Maria's face went red with shame. Stephen quickly went on to making fun of other kids' skiing skills, but his words stuck with Maria. From what she heard, she was the only one who hadn't even tried to ski. What's wrong with me? Maria thought. Why do I have to be different?

Talk About It

- Have you ever let your fears or worries keep you from trying something new? If so, did you feel like you missed out?

- Why don't you think Maria could overcome her fear of skiing?

- Have you ever been made fun of because you wouldn't try something? If so, who made fun of you? How did it make you feel?

When she got home, Maria's mom was making dinner. "Mom, why do I worry all the time? Why am I afraid to do stuff that other kids aren't?" she asked.

Maria's mom wiped her hands on a towel. She put her arm around Maria. "Some people tend to worry more than others, Maria. You've always been that way."

Maria hugged her mom back. "But I want to do what the other kids are doing. Why am I so scared?"

Her mom thought for a second. "It's okay to be worried some of the time. But maybe we should talk to someone if you feel like it's keeping you from the things you really want to do. Let's make an appointment for you."

Maria turned to set the table. She was already feeling a little better. Maybe a doctor would help her to be braver.

Talk About It

- What do you think of Maria's mom's response? Do you think she said the right thing?

- Where do you think the line is between normal worry and anxiety? How can you tell?

Anxiety is overwhelming worry and fear. A person with an anxiety disorder may feel uneasy or be fearful even when there is little reason to be. People with anxiety disorders usually avoid the things that make them worry or feel afraid. This tends to limit them from growing and experiencing new things.

People with anxiety disorders might experience physical symptoms, too, including stomachaches, excessive sweating, or rapid heartbeat. Sometimes these physical symptoms are so disabling that they are called panic attacks. People who suffer from panic attacks feel a sudden intense terror and complete loss of control. Other symptoms include a racing heart, feeling hot, cold, dizzy, or weak, and having difficulty breathing.

If you think you may have an anxiety disorder, talk with a parent or another trusted adult. A doctor can help diagnose you and design a treatment plan. The sooner you get help, the sooner you can start living without fear.

Get Healthy

- If you have fears about doing certain things, try taking them one step at a time. For instance, in Maria's case, she could start by putting on skis. That may be enough for the first day. Another day, she could try riding the chair lift. Each time, add another step until you conquer your fears.

2. Practice using breathing exercises to calm yourself when you become anxious. Sit in a chair with your feet on the floor. Close your eyes and take several deep, slow breaths.

3. Stop comparing yourself to others. It's okay if it takes you a little longer than your friends to work up the courage to try out for the school play or ski down the hill.

The Last Word from Amanda

Adolescence can be a whirlwind of new experiences. Along with these new experiences may come some nervousness or anxiety. It's okay. It's just the little voice in your head saying you're in uncharted territory. If you constantly feel afraid or nervous, this is not normal. If you find that you avoid people, are unable to relax, or are scared of everyday situations, you may have a problem with anxiety.

Anxiety can control your life. Believe me, I know. I had my first panic attack at age 11, and my anxiety grew worse as I got older. When I finally got help, it was as if I had gotten my life back. If you think you may have an anxiety disorder, talk to your parents, another adult, or your doctor. They can get you the help you need.

6

Not Enough Love

At your age, you're too old for your parents' hugs and kisses, right? Wrong! No matter how old you become, you should always be your mom's precious baby, your dad's little girl, or your grandparents' favorite munchkin. They should want to squeeze you close, kiss you, or tell you how special you are to them. This might embarrass you (especially if done in front of your friends), but can you imagine life without it? Imagine never hearing that you're loved. Imagine not being hugged by your parents. Think about how horrible it would be to never hear, "Good job," or "Honey, that's great!"

When parents don't give their child love, affection, and support, they may be emotionally neglecting that child. Emotional neglect can be just as harmful as physical neglect, when a child does not have food or shelter. When a child does not receive the love and attention that she needs, she feels rejected or unworthy of love. Because she hasn't been loved or emotionally cared for, she often doesn't learn how to love or care for others, either. She probably has trouble making and keeping friends. She might become a bully and pick on other people. Maybe you know someone like this . . . someone like Eva.

Eva's Story

> When a child does not receive the love and attention that she needs, she feels rejected or unworthy of love.

Eva and her dad lived alone ever since her mother had died when Eva was two. Eva's dad worked a lot, and when he wasn't working, he was in the garage. Eva knew that her dad loved working on cars. What Eva wasn't sure of was whether her dad loved her.

By the time Eva got up in the morning, her dad had left for work. She made herself cereal for breakfast, packed her lunch, and walked to the bus stop. When she got home from school, she made a snack and watched television. Some nights Eva's dad made dinner, and some nights, he was so late that Eva ate without him. After dinner, her dad would go out to the garage. Sometimes he came in before she went to bed, and sometimes he didn't.

Eva and her dad didn't talk much. Some days they didn't say more than a few words to each other. He never asked her how school went or if she was doing okay. Even on

Eva couldn't remember the last time her dad had hugged her. It was probably when she was little.

nights when Eva's dad cooked, they ate in front of the television.

Eva couldn't remember the last time her dad had hugged her. It was probably when she was little. He had never been affectionate, but since she had become a young adult, he stepped aside if they passed in the hall, as if he were afraid to touch her.

The house always seemed dark and empty. Usually the only sound was the television, or muffled sounds of metal tools clanking in the garage. Eva always felt so alone.

Eva didn't have many friends. Honestly, she didn't have any. The only interaction she had with kids at school was when she picked on them. Some kids tried to be nice to Eva, but it made her uncomfortable. She didn't know how to respond when they tried to make friends. She bullied them until they avoided her like everyone else.

Talk About It

- **Have you ever wondered if your parents love you? What are some of the ways your parents show their love for you?**

- **Do you think Eva's dad really was afraid to touch her? Why or why not?**

- **Do you know someone who is always making fun of other people? Why do you think that person does this?**

One day during lunch break, Eva interrupted a basketball game by stealing the ball. She refused to give it back to the younger kids. A group of kids her age came over to the basketball court.

"Hey, Eva," called Paul, one of the guys in her grade. "Why don't you give back the ball?"

"Make me, Paul," sneered Eva.

Paul shook his head. "What kind of person bullies little kids? Can't you pick on anyone your own size?"

"Like . . . you?" Eva said, and faked throwing the ball at him. Paul flinched, and Eva laughed. "You're just a big wimp, Paul."

"You're the wimp, Eva," Paul said calmly. "You have to steal a little kid's ball just to feel important. No one wants to hang out with you, so you have to play with the little kids. But even they don't want to play with you!"

Talk About It

- Why do you think Eva bullies younger kids?

- Do you think Paul was right to confront Eva? Why or why not?

The entire group walked away, leaving Eva holding the ball. Even the younger kids left. Once again, Eva was alone.

What happened at recess stayed with Eva for the rest of the day. She replayed Paul's words over and over again in her head.

When she got home from school, Eva cooked her dad's favorite meal, lasagna. She wanted to have a real sit-down dinner with him. Maybe they could talk. Maybe he would tell her about her mom. He did that so rarely now.

When Eva's dad came home, Eva surprised him at the door. "Hi, Dad," she said shyly. "I made your favorite dinner." Eva's dad grunted and pushed past her to the kitchen.

He dished up the lasagna and sat down in front of the television. "Umm . . . Dad, I thought we could eat at the table for once. You know, spend some time together," said Eva.

"Eva, quiet. The game is on," her dad said. He didn't even notice when Eva went to her room without eating.

Eva couldn't stop the tears from falling as soon as she closed her bedroom door. She was so confused. When she was mean, no one liked her. When she tried to be nice, nothing changed. Her father's coldness toward her and the episode at lunch played again and again in Eva's mind. Paul's words had hurt her because they were true. She didn't know how to be nice or how to make friends. She couldn't even make her own father like her! All Eva knew was that she was sick of being alone and having no one to talk to.

Talk About It

- **Why do you think Eva made a nice dinner for her dad?**

- **Do you think Eva's father is neglecting her on purpose?**

- **What advice would you give to Eva?**

Just because parents provide their children with food, clothing, and shelter doesn't mean their job is done. Children can be provided for physically but can be neglected when they aren't given the love and guidance they need to grow up to be emotionally healthy. Girls who are emotionally neglected have trouble making connections with other people. This can lead to overwhelming loneliness and isolation.

When people don't get the affection they need from their parents, they begin to believe that they aren't worthy of it. They may be uncomfortable when people care about them. They may react to others with aggression.

Emotionally neglected girls also may seek out the wrong kind of attention. They may engage in risky behavior such as drinking alcohol, taking drugs, or having sex to find the love and attention that is missing from their lives.

If you feel emotionally neglected, try talking to your parents. If things don't get better you need to reach out and find other people such as relatives or adults at school, to be your support network.

Get Healthy

1. If you think your parents or guardians are emotionally neglecting you, tell anothe

adult, such as a teacher, a school counselor, or a religious leader. This adult can help you make a plan for approaching your parents or guardians.

If making friends is difficult for you, make it a point to be nice to everyone. You never know when an opportunity to make a new friend will arise.

Sometimes we have to be our own cheerleaders. Be good to yourself! If you do well on a test, tell yourself that you've done a great job. If you aren't so good at something, tell yourself it's okay and that you'll do better next time. It is important to think positively about yourself, even if you don't always feel positive.

If you don't get attention from your parents, you can seek it from other adults. A relative, a coach, or a counselor could give you the support and guidance you need and deserve.

The Last Word from Amanda

People show love and support in many different ways, but you should never have to question whether your parents love you. If you being emotionally neglected, it is important remember that you haven't done anything cause it. You are a valuable human being who

7

The Breakup

Everyone wants to believe that when two people fall in love and get married, they live happily ever after. Unfortunately, we know that's not always the case. The sad truth is that divorce happens.

Married couples divorce for many different reasons. Some marriages break up because of abuse or addiction. Others break up because the couple has fallen out of love or can't agree on important issues.

No matter the reason for divorce, it is difficult for everyone, especially kids. Sometimes, children blame themselves for the divorce. Girls in this situation must remember that it's not their fault and that their parents still love them.

Adjusting to life after the divorce can be difficult. New custody arrangements can lead to new routines, a new school, a new place to live, or other major changes. Read how Shonda's life changed when her parents broke up.

Shonda's Story

Shonda's parents argued all the time. They couldn't seem to agree on anything. Shonda thought that if one parent said that grass was green, the other would disagree. They tried not to argue around her and her brothers, but Shonda could tell when they had been fighting. She'd walk in on her mom crying, or find her dad sitting with his head in his hands.

Life at home had been uncomfortable for a while.

Shonda didn't know how to help her parents. She tried to do her chores, take care of her brothers, and do well in school, but it didn't seem like what she did mattered. Her parents were still unhappy and kept fighting.

Life at home had been uncomfortable for a while. Shonda spent as much time as she could at friends' houses. One evening when she came home, her parents asked her to talk with them.

"Shonda," her mom said, "your father and I have decided to get a divorce."

The news hit Shonda like a ton of bricks. She was stunned and silent. She knew things weren't good between her parents, but she hadn't thought they'd give up on each other and on their family!

"But you can't get divorced," Shonda said. "What about our family?"

"Your mother and I have decided that this is what's best for the family," said Shonda's dad.

"No, Dad, this is what's best for you! No one asked me what I think," Shonda blurted out. She was angry. How could they just decide this? Didn't they know how this would affect her and her brothers? "How could you guys just give up on our family?" Shonda asked.

"Shonda, we aren't giving up on the family. You'll still see both of us. We'll both be here for you and Michael and Marcus," her mom said gently.

"Your mother and I are the ones who can't make this work, Shonda," said her dad. "This has nothing to do with you or your brothers. We both still love you, and we always will."

That night, Shonda had so many questions running through her head, she couldn't sleep. Did she do something to cause this? Would she have to move? Who would she live with? Where would her brothers live? How would they cope with the divorce? They were only six! Her parents had assured her that everything would be okay, but how could it be? What she did know was that her dad was moving out the next week. She felt as if her world were crashing down around her.

Talk About It

- Have you or a friend had parents who've divorced? How did the divorce affect your life or the life of your friend?

- Why did Shonda feel like her parents were giving up on their family?

- What do you think of the conversation between Shonda and her parents? Do you think her parents told her about the divorce in a good way?

The day her dad moved out, Shonda felt as if she were in a fog. She walked around the house, touching the places where her father's things had been. It was all becoming so real so quickly. Her parents were truly getting divorced. The realization made Shonda's eyes well up with tears.

Shonda worried about where her dad would live, but his new apartment was nice and only a few miles away. There were only two bedrooms, but Shonda's dad said one was hers when she stayed with him. He told her that because she was growing up, she needed privacy and a place of her own. Her brothers would stay on the couch in the living room. Shonda appreciated having her own room. She hugged her dad, and things felt a little more normal.

The day her dad moved out, Shonda felt as if she were in a fog.

A year later, Shonda had mostly adjusted to the new arrangement. She and her brothers lived with their mom during the week, and stayed with their dad most weekends. Both places were calm and peaceful. Shonda was surprised, but she felt relieved that there was no more fighting. Both her parents seemed happier and more relaxed. Shonda still wished her parents could be married and happy. But if that wasn't possible, this felt like the next best thing.

Talk About It

- Why was Shonda worried about where her dad would live?

- Why was it important to Shonda to have her own room at her dad's apartment?

- Why do you think Shonda was surprised about being relieved?

Ask Dr. Robyn

About half of the marriages in the United States end in divorce. Kids who go through divorce are not alone, but they can feel very alone and unsure about the future when their parents divorce. Kids whose parents divorce will have many emotions. They may be angry, fearful, and sad. If the situation at home was especially bad before the divorce, they may even feel relieved. All these feelings are normal.

If your parents are divorced or are divorcing, it's important to remember that it's not your fault. Your parents' decision to divorce is between them and has nothing to do with their love for you.

Divorce brings many changes. It's important that you discuss these changes with your parents and ask them any questions that you have. You should also talk to your parents about how you feel. It is okay to tell them that you feel angry, sad, or afraid. If you don't feel comfortable talking with your parents about how you feel, tell another trusted adult such as a grandparent, a school counselor, or a coach.

Get Healthy

1. You are not responsible for your parents' happiness. Remember that their divorce is

2. Talk to your friends about divorce. If you have friends with divorced parents, ask them how they got through it, and ask if there is anything you can do to help them. If a friend's parents are going through divorce, be there for your friend while she's adjusting.

3. If your parents are divorcing, make sure to talk to them about your feelings. Ask questions so you can prepare yourself for the changes ahead.

4. A divorce is very difficult for your parents, but do not let them put you in the middle of it. Parents should not ask you to take sides or deliver messages to the other parent. Your parents should put aside their differences and talk to each other.

The Last Word from Amanda

If your parents divorce, you may feel hurt, angry, sad, or maybe even relieved. These feelings are normal. The negative feelings may take a long time to go away, but they will. You and your family will adjust to the new changes. You might even find positive things about your parents living separately. Life may not ever be the same after a divorce, but it can still be good.

8

Girl's Best Friend

Do you have a dog or a cat? Maybe you have a bird, a lizard, a guinea pig, or some fish. Animals are great friends. Sometimes, they're better to have around than people. They don't judge, they're good listeners, and they can't disagree with us.

Most of us know what it's like to have an animal friend. Some of us have felt as though our pets are our best friends. Unfortunately, pets don't live as long as we do. What happens when a beloved pet gets sick or is in an accident and dies?

Worse, what do you do when you have a choice? Maybe your pet could live a little while longer, but would be sick and uncomfortable. Could you make the decision to have your pet euthanized? The death of a pet can be a painful, traumatic experience. Just ask Katie.

Katie's Story

Katie had plenty of human friends, but her best friend was a cat named Prince. He had soft gray fur and bright green eyes. Katie's mom had named him Prince because of his regal, proud demeanor.

Katie had a special connection with Prince that no one else in the family had. Prince slept on her bed at night and sat with her when she watched television. Sometimes, Katie felt like Prince was the only one who understood her. She could tell him anything. It seemed silly, but she felt like Prince knew her better than anyone else in the world.

The death of a pet can be a painful, traumatic experience.

When Prince was younger, he was a playful cat. He loved to chase anything that moved. Now that he was older, his reflexes weren't as good. His legs were stiff, and Katie had to lift him onto her bed at night so he could sleep by her.

One day, Katie's dad noticed that Prince wasn't eating very much. He looked like he had lost weight.

Prince had really slowed down—he barely moved from his spot in the sun, and he seemed to be in pain when he went to eat or use the litter box. Katie's parents decided to take him to the vet.

Dr. Garcia, the vet, told Katie and her parents that Prince was dying and there was nothing that could be done. Dr. Garcia suggested that the family think about euthanizing Prince. He explained to Katie that if Prince were euthanized, he would die painlessly. If he weren't, he would slowly starve to death.

Katie was stunned by the news. In the back of her mind, she knew that Prince would die someday, but she wasn't prepared for it to happen yet. She didn't want Prince to feel pain, but she didn't want him to die, either. Katie's parents told Dr. Garcia that they would discuss the options.

Talk About It

- Do you have a pet? How do you feel about your pet?
- Have you ever had to make a tough decision? What did you do?

Katie and her parents had a long talk when they got home. After a lot of crying and hugs and kisses, the family decided that Prince deserved to die without pain. Katie's dad made an appointment to have

Prince euthanized that Saturday. The next few days, Katie cried every time Prince looked at her with his big, green eyes. She held him and murmured to him softly.

"I love you, Prince. I don't want you to die. But I don't want you to hurt anymore. I just hope we're doing the right thing," she told him, tears rolling down her cheeks. Prince purred in answer. It seemed as if he were telling her it was the right decision.

When Saturday came, Katie and her parents said their good-byes to Prince. Katie held him one last time. She didn't know she could hurt so much. Her heart felt as if it were being torn apart.

At the vet's office, Dr. Garcia took Prince from Katie. "Would you like to see Prince when it's over?"

Dr. Garcia asked. Katie nodded. Dr. Garcia took Prince into another room. Ten minutes later, he came back with Prince's lifeless body in his arms. Katie gently stroked his fur.

"Good-bye, Prince. I'll always love you," Katie whispered.

Talk About It

- Have you ever sacrificed something so that someone else could be happy or comfortable? How did it make you feel?

- Have you ever had a pet die? How did you feel when your pet died?

The next day when Katie woke up, Prince wasn't on her bed. The previous day came flooding back, and so did the tears. Katie's mom came in and hugged Katie.

When the tears finally stopped, Katie's mom said, "I have something for you." Katie's mom left and came back with an empty scrapbook and a box of photos.

"I thought we could make a scrapbook of Prince. There are tons of old pictures here, and I think it would be a good memorial to the world's best cat," said Katie's mom.

A week later, Katie and her parents sat with the scrapbook

"Good-bye, Prince. I'll always love you," Katie whispered.

and the photos. Katie pasted photos into the book and wrote a story about each picture. She was amazed by how much one cat had touched her life. She was still terribly sad that Prince was gone, but at the same time, she was happy to have so many good memories of him.

Talk About It

- Why do you think Katie's mom suggested making a scrapbook of Prince?

- Have you ever done something in memory of a pet? If so, what?

- Do you think it would be a good idea for Katie to get another cat right away? Why or why not?

Ask Dr. Robyn

Pets can become part of the family, so when they die, it can be like losing a friend or family member. When a pet dies, you will go through a period of time called grief. Grief is the normal reaction to a loss. During this process, you will feel intense sadness and may even feel angry or guilty. You may cry a lot, may not feel like eating, or may not be able to sleep. These feelings and actions are natural and normal.

Grieving takes a different amount of time for each person, but make sure to let your feelings out. Pushing away your feelings or trying to ignore them only makes the grieving process longer. Acknowledging your feelings is a step toward accepting the loss of your pet.

Talk to friends who have lost pets. Ask your parents about their pets that have died. These people can comfort you and tell you what to expect in the coming days and weeks.

Get Healthy

1. Honor your pet in a special way. Make a scrapbook of pictures and stories. Plant a tree or a flower. Have a family memorial service where you all talk about happy memories of your pet.

2. Talk to others who may have known your pet, such as your friends, grandparents, and neighbors. They may have funny or sweet stories about your pet that you don't know about.

3. Refrain from getting a new pet right away. It may be tempting to try to replace your lost pet to stop the emotional pain, but it usually doesn't work. Allow yourself time to grieve before bringing a new animal into the family. It's not fair to the new pet to become part of your family when you're not emotionally ready for it.

4. If you were emotionally close to your pet, it's natural to grieve. Don't let anyone tell you it was "just a pet" so you shouldn't be upset.

The Last Word from Amanda

Losing a friend, human or animal, is very difficult. You will miss your pet for a long time after he or she is gone. Your home may feel different, and your heart may feel a little empty. This sadness is a natural part of grief. Even though it may hurt at first, you will soon find comfort in your fond memories. Each animal is special and different, and when the time is right, you will be able to welcome a new pet into your home.

9
A Tragic End

We've learned that depression is a difficult emotional disorder that makes people feel sad and hopeless. Some people get help for their depression and learn to cope with it. Unfortunately, some people are so disabled by their depression that they believe there is no help for them. The depression and sadness make them feel as if their lives are worthless. Sometimes, these people try to commit suicide. And sometimes, they succeed.

The suicide rate among preteen girls is climbing. How do you know if one of your friends is in danger? There are warning signs to watch for. People who are suicidal often talk about death or committing suicide. They may talk about feeling worthless or hopeless. They tend to pull away from friends or family, and may quit doing activities they used to enjoy. They may have trouble sleeping, or they might sleep all the time. Their grades may drop. Sometimes, people who are contemplating suicide give away their possessions. Beth didn't see these signs in her friend, Heather.

Beth's Story

Beth and Heather had been best friends since they were five. They lived next door to each other, rode the same bus to school, and spent evenings doing homework together. Beth and Heather both played clarinet, loved the same music, and giggled over the same boys.

Heather was quiet and got good grades in school. Heather's family life, though, was a mess. Her parents were alcoholics and fought constantly. Heather's older brother, Ross, was rumored to be on drugs and was always in trouble. Heather hated being at home, so the girls usually went to Beth's house after school.

Heather hated being at home, so the girls usually went to Beth's house after school.

One morning at the bus stop, Beth noticed that Heather's eye looked puffy. It was also caked with makeup, as if she were hiding something. Beth asked what happened to Heather's eye, but Heather pretended not to hear.

"Heather, did Ross do that to you again?" Beth asked. Ross had a history of hitting whoever got in his way. Heather nodded.

"You should really tell someone about this. I can't believe your parents didn't do anything!"

Heather's eyes started to tear up. "No one cares about what he does to me. They won't even care when I'm dead."

"I care!" exclaimed Beth. "I bet the school counselor would care."

"No, he wouldn't. Besides, if Ross found out that I told on him, he'd hurt me worse. He's crazy," Heather whispered.

Talk About It

- **Has someone ever threatened to hurt you if you told on him or her? What did you do in that situation?**

- **Do you think Beth should tell the school counselor what happened to Heather?**

The next week, the girls worked on an English assignment in Beth's room. "We have to write about our favorite place. What's yours?" Beth asked Heather, noticing the bruises on Heather's arms. Heather had been more quiet than usual lately.

"I think my favorite place would be heaven," said Heather quietly.

"Well, maybe, but you've never been there," Beth joked.

"Not yet," Heather mumbled.

"I think Ms. Graham means our favorite place on Earth," said Beth. "Come on, what's yours?"

"Who cares?" said Heather. "It's a stupid assignment." She slid off the bed and put on her jacket.

"Well, it's due tomorrow and worth 10 percent of our grade," said Beth.

"I'm not writing the dumb paper. I don't have a favorite place, and I don't care about my stupid grade." Heather walked out of Beth's room. A few seconds later, the front door slammed. What was up with Heather? English was her favorite class, and she loved writing.

The next day, Heather didn't show up to English class. She wasn't on the bus ride home, either. That night, Beth called Heather's house. She could hear Heather's mom cursing in the background.

"Where were you today?" asked Beth. "The bus had to leave without you."

"Um . . . I walked home," mumbled Heather.

"Really? Why?" asked Beth, surprised.

"I don't know. I just needed to be alone," replied Heather.

"Is everything okay?

"I guess. Whatever," said Heather.

"Do you want to talk?" asked Beth.

The next day, Heather didn't show up to English class.

"Nah, I'm kinda tired. I'm going to bed," replied Heather.

"All you do is sleep, you lazy pig," Beth overheard Ross say.

Heather managed to avoid Beth for the next week. She walked to and from school by herself. If she showed up to class, she looked down and didn't talk to anyone.

Talk About It

- **What did Heather mean when she said her favorite place would be heaven?**

- **Why do you think Heather blew off the English assignment?**

- **What might be some reasons Heather is avoiding Beth?**

The next day, Mr. Gussert, the band teacher, asked to talk to Beth after practice. He congratulated her on being the new first-seat clarinet.

Beth looked at him, confused. "But Heather is first seat."

"Heather quit band this morning. I thought you would know, since you two are so close," Mr. Gussert said. He frowned.

We used to be close, Beth thought. What had happened to their friendship? Why had Heather quit band without even telling her? They told each other everything, or so she had thought.

After dinner, Beth walked next door, determined to find out what was wrong with Heather. When Heather opened the door, Beth was surprised at how pale she was.

"I heard you quit band. How could you quit? And why didn't you tell me?" Beth asked.

Heather gave Beth a sad smile. "You can be first clarinet now," said Heather.

"I don't care about being first clarinet. Heather, what's wrong? I'm really worried about you."

Heather sighed. "I'm fine. I've just been a little tired lately." Beth heard a crash and a string of slurred curses from inside the house.

"Hey, I gotta go, okay?" Heather turned to go inside.

"Heather, wait! Can't we talk?" begged Beth.

Heather looked into Beth's pleading eyes. "Maybe tomorrow, okay?" She stepped inside the house and closed the door.

The next day at school, Beth was called to the principal's office. Beth walked down the hall, her heart pounding. She opened the door, and saw her mom and the school's guidance counselor, Mr. Yung. Beth's mom was crying.

"Mom, what's going on? Why are you crying?" Beth asked.

Mr. Yung sighed. "Beth, I have some very bad news to tell you. I know you and Heather were very close. I'm so very sorry, but Heather died this morning. Her mother found an empty container of pills by her bed."

Beth drew in a quick breath, and her body went numb. She thought she was going to be sick. How could this have happened? Why would her best friend have committed suicide?

Talk About It

- Were there any warning signs that Heather was planning to commit suicide?

- Do you think Beth could have done anything to stop Heather from committing suicide? Why or why not?

If you think a friend may be suicidal, ask her if she is contemplating suicide. This may be a difficult conversation to start, but it may be the most important talk you and your friend ever have. Listen carefully to your friend. If she has considered suicide, take her thoughts or plans seriously. Tell her that you are worried about her, that you care, and that she is not alone.

Your friend might tell you to keep her plans a secret, but you can't. Tell a trusted adult about your concerns right away. If you fear that your friend might be in immediate danger, stay with her and call 911 or a suicide crisis line. You can find suicide crisis phone numbers online, in your local phone book, or at the back of this book.

The death of a friend is extremely difficult under any circumstances, but may be even more emotional if that person kills herself. The people she leaves behind often feel very guilty. They think they should have been able to stop her somehow. It's important to remember that no matter how guilty you feel, your friend's death is not your fault. You cannot control other people, and you cannot take responsibility for their actions.

If a friend commits suicide, you may go through a process of grieving that may take weeks, months, or even years. Everyone grieves differently and in her own time. If you find your grief process exceptionally difficult, it may help to talk to a therapist or to join a support group for suicide survivors.

Get Healthy

1. If you see suicide warning signs in a friend, tell a trusted adult right away. Your quick action may save your friend's life.

2. Talk to your friends about suicide. Make a pact to be there for each other if someone is suicidal. Sometimes, just knowing that you have a person to talk to is enough to make you feel better.

3. Sometimes people feel so depressed about losing their loved ones that they fall into deep depression. They may even begin contemplating suicide. If this happens to you, get help right away.

The Last Word from Amanda

The suicide of a friend can be one of the most difficult things a person can go through. By knowing the warning signs, hopefully you will be able to help your friend before it gets to that point. If a friend does commit suicide, it is important to remember that it is not your fault. Your grieving process may be long, but eventually you will enjoy and embrace life

10

Losing Dad

What is the worst possible thing you can imagine? Many girls may say the death of a parent. We all know our parents will die eventually. If we are lucky, they will live to see our children and maybe our grandchildren. But sometimes, parents die too early. People can die slowly from things such as cancer or a terminal disease. This gives us a chance to prepare ourselves and say good-bye. Other times, people die in an instant, leaving us stunned.

No matter how a parent dies, it can be one of the most intensely painful times in a person's life. The death of a parent is especially traumatic to kids. Autumn knew her life would never be the same.

Autumn's Story

Autumn was a normal 12-year-old girl. She had a few close friends, did well in school, and was one of the best basketball players in her middle school. Autumn lived in the suburbs with her parents and her eight-year-old brother, Chris.

Winter was always a fun time of year for Autumn's family. They all went skiing, sledding, or snowmobiling almost every weekend. Autumn loved the snow, and she would bundle up and make snowmen or snow forts with her brother. Sometimes, their dad would join them, throwing them in snowbanks and letting them bury him up to his head in the snow.

No matter how a parent dies, it can be one of the most intensely painful times in a person's life.

One Monday morning after a fun winter weekend, the area was hit with a snowstorm. Autumn watched as the snow blew down, covering the ground with a fresh, white blanket. School was delayed for two hours, so she was taking her time with breakfast.

The phone rang, and Autumn's mom answered it. Autumn watched as her mom's face went almost as white as the snow. She immediately knew something was wrong. Autumn's mom sank into a kitchen chair.

"Mom, what's wrong?" cried Autumn. Chris came into the kitchen.

"Chris, please come sit down," said their mom, shakily. She grabbed Autumn and Chris's hands.

"Kids, your father has been in a car accident. He died on the way to the hospital."

The three of them hugged each other tightly, not knowing what to do or say. They clung to each other and cried.

Talk About It

- **Have you had a parent, a grandparent, or someone else close to you die? If so, how did you react when you found out?**

- **If you've had someone close to you die, what feelings did you experience? If you haven't, how do you think you would feel?**

Autumn couldn't believe that her father was dead. He had been so alive when he had kissed her before leaving that morning. She could smell his after-shave and his warm scent. She could see him putting on his big winter coat and thick gloves before heading outside. She wished she could remember more. She wanted to fix every little thing in her memory.

Within a few hours, her grandparents, aunts, uncles, and cousins began to flood into the house. They kissed Autumn and Chris, told them it would be okay, and held their mother as she cried. Autumn just wanted to be alone. She went to her room and lay

down on her bed. She wasn't tired, but she felt numb, and her head buzzed with thoughts. Chris came into Autumn's room and lay down beside her. Usually, Autumn and Chris argued and teased each other, but these weren't normal circumstances. Autumn put her arm around her brother.

"What's going to happen to us, Autumn? What are we going to do without Dad?" he asked.

"I don't know, Chris. I really don't know," she said, shaking her head.

The next few days passed in a blur. Family and neighbors brought over food that no one was hungry for. Even some of Autumn's friends stopped by. She didn't know what to say, so she just nodded when they told her they were sorry and accepted their hugs.

Autumn's grandma took her and Chris shopping for clothes to wear to the funeral. Autumn usually loved to shop, but this time she just bought the first black dress she saw in her size.

Talk About It

- If you have had someone close to you die, what things do you remember most about them?
- Why do you think Autumn wanted to be alone?

The wake and the funeral were difficult. Autumn still couldn't believe that it was her father in the casket. His skin looked like it was made out of wax, and his hair was combed wrong.

Before the wake, Autumn's mom had asked if she wanted to put anything in the casket to be buried with her dad. Autumn immediately ran to get her favorite stuffed animal, a white puppy that her dad had gotten her for her fourth birthday. Autumn had slept with it until last year. She placed the white puppy by her dad's shoulder.

"Here, Dad. You gave me Snowball to watch over me at night. Now he can watch over you," she said.

After the funeral, life seemed to go back to normal, but it wasn't normal. Autumn returned to

school, but her friends got quiet when she was around. Autumn played basketball, but her heart wasn't in it. She couldn't force herself to play in the snow with her brother, and the family began staying indoors on the weekends.

Nights were the hardest. At night Autumn thought about what she would give to

After the funeral, life seemed to go back to normal, but it wasn't normal.

see her dad one last time, to hear his laugh, to feel his scratchy face against her cheek, to tell him she loved him. Some nights, she crawled into bed with her mom, and the two of them held each other and cried until they fell asleep. Some nights, Chris would climb in, too, falling asleep clutching his dad's pillow.

Talk About It

- **Have you ever been to a wake or a funeral? Were you able to approach the casket? How did the funeral make you feel?**

- **Why do you think Autumn's friends were quiet when she was around?**

- **If a friend lost one of her parents, how would you comfort him or her?**

Autumn missed her dad so much it hurt. Sometimes her chest felt like it would burst open, revealing her broken heart. Autumn was surprised by the intensity of her anguish. It was like nothing she had ever felt before. Sometimes it felt like she was going crazy. Autumn wondered if she would ever be able to smile, laugh, or be happy again.

Talk About It

- Have you ever been in so much emotional pain that your body hurt, too? What did it feel like?

- Do you think that Autumn will ever be happy again? Can you think of something that might make her feel better?

- What would you say to Autumn about dealing with her dad's death?

If you lose a parent, you will feel intense emotions unlike anything you have felt before. You will probably feel shocked, extremely sad, anxious, worried, confused, or angry. Many people feel guilty. This is natural, but it is important to remember that the death is not your fault. Some people feel numb, or feel as though they are living outside of their bodies.

People can have physical symptoms, too. They may have trouble sleeping or lose their appetites. It may be difficult to participate in your usual activities, but it is important to try. These routines can keep you from isolating yourself from others and letting your grief control you.

While much of life will return to normal routines soon, the grieving process may last for months or even years. People grieve in different ways, but the important thing is to let your feelings out. You may not be able to talk about your parent right away, and that's okay. You may feel more comfortable writing in a journal or drawing pictures.

While it may seem that you will never be happy again, you will. You may have moments of sadness, but happy memories of your parent will replace the intense hurt. You have not forgotten about your parent. You are beginning

1. A memorial can help you grieve and relive good memories about the person you have lost. Collect photos of your loved one, make a quilt from the person's clothes, or plant a tree in his or her honor.

2. Attend a support group for people who are grieving over loved ones. It is a safe environment to express your emotions.

3. Talk about your parent when you are able to. It will help you heal. Do something special to remember your parent on holidays, birthdays, and other occasions.

The Last Word from Amanda

Dealing with the death of a parent is one of the most difficult things for anyone to have to do. You may be tempted to try to be strong for your surviving parent or siblings, but you need to grieve as well. Families can grieve together and help each other heal.

While grieving is normal and may take a long time, sometimes people need a little extra help. If you have been grieving for a while and things aren't getting better, you may be depressed. If you feel extremely down, can't concentrate, or think about hurting yourself, talk to a trusted adult. You may benefit from talking to a counselor who specializes in grief therapy.

A Second Look

I hope that you never have to deal with any of the emotional issues in this book. However, I hope that this book has given you the knowledge and empowerment to know what to do if faced with these situations.

It may not seem like it at first, but the topics in this book are all linked. Depression and anxiety can lead to suicide. Suicide, grief, and emotional neglect can cause depression and anxiety, as can major changes, such as moving or divorce. People with depression, anxiety, and ADHD are more likely to abuse substances than people without these disorders, and people who abuse substances often end up being depressed or anxious.

While some of the stories you have just read are sad and tragic, there is reason to feel hope. There is help for those who want it. Doctors can help diagnose depression, anxiety, and ADHD. They can provide treatment plans that include medication and therapy or alternative methods. Those who are grieving the loss of a friend or family member can get counseling and attend support groups to help them cope. There are even support groups for children of divorced parents.

The biggest help to anyone experiencing emotional issues is having a group of close friends and family for support. Everyone needs people to talk to, people to listen, and a shoulder to cry on. Surround yourself with people who love you and care about you, and make sure to love and care for them, too. Rely on these people when times get tough.

If you are experiencing anything like the people in this book, you need to talk to someone, whether it is a friend, a parent, a coach, or a guidance counselor. You are not alone, and these issues are not ones that can be dealt with by yourself. Please get the support and help that you need and deserve. You will be glad that you did.

XOXO,
Amanda

Pay It Forward

Remember, a healthful life is about balance. Now that you know how to walk that path, pay it forward to a friend or even to yourself! Remember the Get Healthy tips throughout this book, and then take these steps to get healthy and get going.

• Get help if you are experiencing depression, anxiety, a lack of concentration, emotional neglect, substance abuse, or intense grief. Talk to a trusted adult such as a parent, a school counselor, a doctor, or a religious leader.

• Talk to your friends about emotional issues. Make a pact to always be there for each other if these issues arise. Sometimes, just knowing that someone is there to listen can make you feel better.

• Remember that you have done nothing wrong to deserve depression, anxiety, ADHD, or emotional neglect. You are a worthwhile, valuable person who deserves love and support.

• Stay away from alcohol, drugs, and prescription medicine that is not yours. Abusing substances will make emotional problems worse, not better. Substances also alter a person's judgment, causing people to take risks and make poor choices.

- Think positively! Research shows that looking for the good in life can help people cope better in difficult situations and improve their overall health. The more you practice positive thinking, the more natural it becomes.

- Your emotional health is closely tied to your physical health. Eating a nutritious diet and getting plenty of exercise and sleep can go a long way in helping you cope with emotional issues.

- Make a list of things you enjoy doing. If you find yourself feeling down, look at this list, choose an activity, and do it!

- Face grief head-on. When dealing with the death of a loved one, you will experience many raw, intense emotions. Dealing with these emotions can be a frightening thing, but pushing them down or ignoring them causes them to reappear in other situations, often when it isn't appropriate.

- Remember that things like emotional neglect, your parents' divorce, or the suicide of a friend are not your fault. You cannot control others or take responsibility for their actions.

Additional Resources

Select Bibliography

Olson, Ginny. *Teenage Girls: Exploring Issues Adolescent Girls Face and Strategies to Help Them.* Grand Rapids, MI: Zondervan, 2006.

Pipher, Mary Bray. *Reviving Ophelia: Saving the Selves of Adolescent Girls.* New York: Putnam, 1994.

Zailckas, Koren. *Smashed: Story of a Drunken Girlhood.* New York: Penguin Books, 2005.

Further Reading

McLinden, Shannon. *The Me Nobody Knew.* Minneapolis, MN: First Avenue Editions, 1997.

Sjoqvist, Suzanne, and Margaret Myers. *Still Here With Me: Teenagers and Children on Losing a Parent.* London: Jessica Kingsley Publishers, 2006.

Taylor, John F. *The Survival Guide for Kids with ADD or ADHD.* Minneapolis, MN: Free Spirit Publishing, 2006.

Web Sites

To learn more about handling emotional issues, visit ABDO Publishing Company online at **www.abdopublishing.com**. Web sites about handling emotional issues are featured on our Book Links page. These links are routinely monitored and updated to provide the most current information available.

For More Information

For more information on this subject, contact or visit the following organizations.

Depression and Bipolar Support Alliance

730 North Franklin Street, Suite 501, Chicago, IL 60654
800-826-3632
www.dbsalliance.org
The Depression and Bipolar Support Alliance is a national nonprofit organization that works to prevent and manage mental illness.

National Institute of Drug Abuse and Addiction

6001 Executive Boulevard, Room 5213
Bethesda, MD 20892-9561
301-443-1124
www.drugabuse.gov; http://teens.drugabuse.gov/
This government agency provides information for teens about preventing drug abuse.

National Suicide Prevention Lifeline

800-273-8255
www.suicidepreventionlifeline.com
This 24-hour, toll-free hotline is available to anyone in a suicidal crisis.

SAVE—Suicide Awareness Voices of Education

8120 Penn Avenue South, Suite 470
Bloomington, MN 55431
952-946-7998
www.save.org
A nonprofit organization, SAVE strives to raise awareness of depression and suicide through education.

Glossary

addiction
The need of a substance (such as drugs or alcohol) to function.

anxiety
An abnormal and overwhelming sense of fear or worry.

cope
To deal with and attempt to overcome problems and difficulties.

depression
A mood disorder that causes sadness, feelings of dejection and hopelessness, and, sometimes, suicidal thoughts.

diagnose
To recognize a disease by its signs and symptoms.

emotional neglect
Failure to provide love, affection, security, and emotional support.

euthanasia
The practice of killing a hopelessly sick or injured animal in a painless way.

extracurricular
Relating to organized student activities (such as sports, drama club, and others).

grief
Intense distress caused by the loss of something (such as the death of a loved one).

hyperactivity
The state or condition of moving or fidgeting excessively.

impulsivity
The state or condition of acting quickly, often without thinking.

inattention
The state or condition of failing to focus.

isolate
To separate from another.

memorial
An action to remind you of someone or something.

pact
An agreement or promise.

puberty
The period of time when males and females become physically sexually mature.

therapy
Treatment of a mental, bodily, or behavioral disorder.

traumatic
Shocking or upsetting.

Index

ADHD, 18–27
anxiety, 26, 29, 48–55
anxiety disorder, 48–49,
    54–55
attention, 18, 21, 22, 26,
    57, 64, 65

behavior disorder, 18–19,
    26

custody, 67, 70

death
    friend, 82–91
    parent, 92–101
    pet, 74–81
depression, 26, 29,
    38–47, 48, 82, 91
divorce, 10, 66–73

emotional neglect, 56–65
euthanasia, 75, 76, 77–78
experimentation, 36

family, 10, 11, 14, 16, 18,
    37, 46, 47, 49, 68,
    73, 75, 76, 80, 81,
    83, 93, 95, 97
forgetfulness, 19, 26
friends, 10, 11–12, 13,
    16, 17, 18, 20–21,
    24, 37, 38, 39, 40,
    46, 47, 48, 49, 50,
    55, 56, 57, 58, 62,
    65, 67, 73, 74, 75,
    80, 81, 82–83, 87,
    88, 90–91, 93, 95, 97

grief, 80, 81, 90–91,
    100–101

hopelessness, 39, 82–83
hyperactivity, 18, 26

impatience, 18
impulsivity, 26

love, 56–57, 64–65, 66,
    68, 72, 74, 77, 78,
    97, 101

medication, 24, 27, 29,
    31–35, 36–37
moving, 10–17

nervousness, 31, 48–49,
    54–55
new life, 13, 70

restlessness, 18, 26

self-esteem, 64
substance abuse, 28–37
suicide, 46, 82–91

therapy, 24, 27, 47, 101

worry. *See* anxiety
worthlessness, 39, 47,
    82–83

About the Author

Amanda Doering Tourville has written more than 40 books for children. This book was her most intensive, personal project. She would like to thank her five strong, beautiful nieces for being her inspiration during the writing of this manuscript. Amanda is greatly honored to write for young people and hopes that they will learn to love reading and learning as much as she does. When not writing, Amanda enjoys traveling, photography, and hiking. She lives in Minnesota with her husband and guinea pig.

Photo Credits